POLICE SLANG

Compiled by Charles Harris

ABSON BOOKS LONDON

5 Sidney Square London E1 2EY
Tel 020 7790 4737
Fax 020 7790 7346
email absonbooks@aol.com
web www.absonbooks.co.uk

ABSON BOOKS LONDON
First published June 2010
© Charles Harris
Designed by Bill Vickers

Printed by Ashford Colour Press UK
ISBN 978 0902920 866

INTRODUCTION

Police Slang illuminates the darker sides of life with brevity, irony, and a razor sharp dose of reality, opening a new and unexpected window to the world as seen by the men and women who are at the sharp end of crime.

Police slang calls it as cops see it, and few remain unspared. Sometimes this means a thousand three-letter acronyms, official, brief and to the point. At other times, an acid dry humour can be heard in the way uniformed police refer to those in plain clothes and vice versa, and in the way they all talk about new initiatives - see the terms for PCSO (Police Community Support Officer) - and in the way they refer to civilians, judges and members of rival police forces.

While cop shows and crime novels are as popular as ever this is, to say the least, a challenging time to be in the British police where they face more pressures than ever from media scrutiny and public questioning - and from new ways of working, more paperwork and more rules. The slang the police use reflects all of this.

If you ever wondered what cops are saying when they talk among themselves, or have wanted to follow the quick backchat of a TV cop show, or like to read police novels or true crime, then this little book is for you.
It is a backstage pass to the real "canteen culture" that lies behind the public face of the police.

Charles Harris

100 yard hero	Person happy to abuse the police from a distance
AA	Activity Analysis
Accelerated promotion	see HPDS
ACPO	Association of Chief Police Officers
Advice	Strong physical persuasion (Merseyside)
Ambo	Ambulance (W Midlands)
Angler	Uses a pole like a fishing rod to steal from easily accessible windows
ANPR	Automatic Number Plate Recognition
Area	The Metropolitan Police divides London into three Areas, North West, North East and South, especially for the major crime units
Back door	Nearest pub to the police station
Backshift	Late turn, 2-10pm shift (Strathclyde) See also early turn, late turn, day, EP

Bad call	Incorrect assessment of the attractions of the opposite sex. See also Good call
Bag dropper	Steals from handbags (Strathclyde)
Bamber, to do a	Make a mistake
Bang up	Send to jail
Banter	Describing a close-knit team. as *"They've got good banter that lot"*
BANTER	Big Arse No Tits Easily Rattled
Bar office	Police station reception officer (Strathclyde)
BCU	Borough Command Unit
Beak	Magistrate
BEM	Business Excellence Model
Big house	Prison
BINGO	Bollocks I'm Not Getting Out, as in BINGO seat at back of a police carrier where the laziest officer sits
Bizzy	Police Officer (Merseyside)

Black rats	Traffic police (from the idea that black rats don't eat their own kind). It's alleged off duty traffic officers used to put a picture of a black rat in their rear window to avoid being pulled over for speeding, etc. See Rat
Black rover	Warrant card, when used to get free travel on bus, tube or train. See also GTP
Blahing	Boasting about previous jobs
Blues & twos	Siren and flashing lights
Blunkett's Babes	Police Community Support Officers, set up by then Home Secretary David Blunkett
Bobby	Police constable
Body	Client who is either under arrest or very soon will be
Body set	Recorder taped to body of undercover officer. See also Wire
BONGO	Books On, Never Goes Out; Office-bound officer. See also BINGO, Station cat, Olympic flame, Olympic torch
Borough Command	Central command of a borough. In London, each borough is a single police administrative unit under a Commander (Met)

Borough Control	Communications room at central police station of a borough (obsolete) see also IBO (Met)
Boss	Senior officer (any rank above Inspector) See also Guv, Guv'nor
Box	Witness stand in court
Boy racer	Young member of the public with car, not necessarily his own
BPA	Black Police Association
Bramshill	Police Training College for senior officers
Bridewell	Charge room and cells (Merseyside)
Brief	(a) Solicitor or barrister, (b) Police officer's warrant card
Brighton knockers	Door to door con-men
Bubble someone	Give someone away, implicating an associate
Buck	Tearaway, villain, yob (Merseyside)
Burst	Confess; get to confess (Strathclyde)
Butterfly	Officer who makes energetic movements to achieve nothing very much and gets rapidly promoted

C & D	Complaints and Discipline – Internal investigations, given different names in different regions. See also DPS
C-3PO	Police Community Support Officer
Canteen cowboy	Officer who knows it all & is happy to ensure others know it
Canteen culture	Unofficial values and beliefs of officers, as shared in the canteen & a source of friction with the higher authorities
Carrot cruncher	County Police Officer (Met). See also Metrocomicals
CAT	(a) Community Action Team, (b) Counter Assault Team
CBF	Combined Benevolent Fund
CBT	Computer Based Training
CHAV	Council House And Vermin, Council House And Violent etc, difficult person of lower social index
CHIMPS	Can't Help In Most Police Situations; Police Community Support Officers
Chink-chink	Call put out on radio to intimate that it's time to return to base for hot beverages (from sound of cups rattling when being filled)
CHIS	Covert Human Intelligence Source – an informant

Choirboys	HM Customs and Excise
CID	(a) Criminal Investigation Department, plain clothes detectives (b) Criminals in Disguise (substitute another C word as preferred) (Uniformed branch)
Claret	Blood
Click	Small street gang. See also Crew
Clock	(a) see, recognise, spot (b) hit. Both meanings probably from earlier slang: clock (noun) meaning face
Clothes hanger	Useless or ineffective officer. See also uniform carrier
Cluster	Call that results in a messy, difficult and mostly pointless amount of work
CO19 (formerly SO19)	Specialist Firearms Command, deals with guns and armed support for police units
Cock	Person who gives an officer something (often a publican providing drinks)
Code blue	Death involved
Con	(a) convicted criminal (b) confidence trick (c) constable (Merseyside)
Contact therapy	Physical restraint with use of fists and/or feet

Cook the books	Make an area appear safer to the public than it really is. See also Not Carnival Related
Cough, cough up	Confess
Cough job	Confession
Cowards Castle	Strathclyde Police HQ (Strathclyde) See also Kremlin
Crew	Street gang. See also Click
CRIMINT	Criminal intelligence database
CS	Canister Spray
CSI	Crime Scene Investigator (formerly SOCO)
Cuff	(a) Handcuff (b) Deal politely with a victim or informant who has no real grievance or information
Cush	Savings for an emergency
CV job	Case likely to result in a significant number of convictions, good for the career
D and D	Drunk and disorderly

Day	Day patrol 10am-6pm (Merseyside)
DC	Detective Constable
Death message	News to be delivered that someone close has died
Department	CID (Met) See also The Firm
DILLIGAFF	Does It Look Like I Give A Flying F*ck?
Do you take Warrant card	Unofficial practice of obtaining services or goods at reduced or no payment. Now said to be done away with
Docket	Police file
Domestic	Incident between partners which can end with both attacking the PC attending
Done it in	Late for a shift, as *"I've done it in again"*
Donna	Female chav (from Doner Kebab)
Double-Bubble	Double-time overtime payment
DPS	Directorate of Professional Standards, investigates suspected corruption of police officers (Met)
Drink, a	Bribe money

Drop a bollock	Make a procedural mistake - source of stress as this can lead to suspects getting off on a technicality
Drum	Club, home, any place to be raided. See also Spin, Turn over
DS	Detective Sergeant
DVI	Disaster Victim Identification
DWE	Driving While Elderly
Dwell the box	Wait around in location for something to happen
Early turn	First shift of the day, normally 6am-2pm
EDP	Emotionally Disturbed Person
End	Share of crime proceeds, as *"He got his end"*
End of sports	Suspect arrested (Gwent)
Enforcer	Battering ram for entering locked premises. See also Rammit
EP	Early patrol 6am-2pm (Merseyside)
EPF	Extended Police Family

ESSO	Every Saturday/Sunday Off
Face	Known villain
Factory	Police station
FAGI	False Alarm, Good Intent – reported incident by member of public which turned out to be innocuous (Strathclyde)
Feel a collar	Arrest
FIFO	Fit In Or F*ck Off
FIGMO	F*ck It, Got My Orders
Filth	Police (especially Detectives)
Fire in (someone)	Give up accomplice in return for lenient treatment, as *"If you fire in your mates we'll reduce the charges"* (Strathclyde)
First aid kit	Evidence kept ready to plant on a suspect (allegedly)
Fit up	Frame, incriminate on a false charge, enhance the evidence. See also Noble cause corruption, Verbal
Floater	Body found in water

13

FLUB	Fat Lazy Useless Bastard. See also Uniform Carrier
FME	Force Medical Examiner (examines health of police and suspects)
Force feeding	Canteen catering
Front	Owner of a business with a clean record who covers for the real criminal owner
FTA	Failed To Appear or Failed To Attend
FUBAR	F*cked Up Beyond All Recognition
FUMTU	F*cked Up More Than Usual
Gaff	(a) place, home (b) money
Gate fever	Emotion shown by a prisoner finishing a sentence
GDC	God Damn Civvy, non-police person
Gear	Drugs
Geemarc	Telephone recorder
Get a drink	Given money by a criminal

Ghosties	Police team that breaks through doors (from the film 'Ghostbuster')
GI	General Information
Give a tug	Stop a member of the public, as *"give him a tug"*
Go bandit	Decide to plead not guilty
Go dark	Go bad, turn to crime
Going up the road	Going to prison
Golden hook	Corrupt practice of taking a broken down car to a garage that gives a percentage of the bill to the Police Officer concerned
Good call	(a) Police presence rightly requested (b) Correct assessment of attractions of a member of the opposite sex. See also Bad call
GP car	General Patrol car. Plain car without police markings
Graft	Corruption, backhander, bribe
Grass	Inform, Informer. See also Supergrass, CHIS, Snout, Snitch
Gravel rash	Accidental damage to face of prisoner when taken to ground
Griff	Full facts
Grip the rails	Stand in the dock (as a defendant)

GTP	Good To Police, offering goods or services cheap or free
Gunship	Unmarked car containing armed officers
Gurkha	Officer who doesn't make arrests *(from "Gurkhas don't take prisoners")*
Guv, guvnor	Inspector or above, officer who doesn't earn overtime
Gypsy's warning	A quiet word in someone's ear – now out of fashion, politically incorrect
HAT car	Transports the HAT team
HAT team	Homicide Assessment Team, sent out first to scene of a murder or other serious crime
Hats and bats	Helmets and riot sticks
Heavy mob	Customs and Excise
Helmet	Uniformed police person
Hendon	Metropolitan police training school. See also Bramshill
HOLMES	Home Office Large Major Enquiry System. Computerised system for aiding detective teams on major cases

HORT/1	Ticket given to a driver to produce licence etc at a police station within 7 days
HOSTYDS	Hollow Spike Tyre Deflation System – laid across a road it does what it says on the can
HPDS	High Potential Development Scheme for fast-tracking officers with high rank potential (formerly known as Accelerated Promotion)
HVP	High Visibility Policing
IBO	Integrated Borough Operations. Department in a borough that liaises with the centralised despatch system in London to add local information to an emergency call. See also Metcall
IC 1	Identity Code 1, white person – The IC is used by the police to refer to a person's visual appearance without it being obvious if they are overheard (see the following)
IC 2	Mediterranean or Hispanic person
IC 3	Afro-Caribbean person
IC 7	Official: Unknown ethnic origin, alien. Unofficial: (a) Ginger person (b) Frequent user of sunbeds

Ice	Cocaine
Ice cream habit	Occasional recreational drugs use
IKEA	I Know Everything Already
Innit	Chav, as *"He's a right innit"*
IP	Impending Prosecution
IPCC	Independent Police Complaints Commission
IPLDP	Initial Police Learning and Development Programme (referred to as Ipildip)
IRV	Incident Response Vehicle
Jack	Plain clothes officer. Also Big City Jack, self-important plain clothes officer in big city force
JAFLO	Just Another F*cking Liaison Officer
JAFO	Just Another F*cking Observer
Jam jar	Car
Jam sandwich	Police car (from the red line down the middle)

Job	Police employment
Job-pissed	Workaholic
Jobby	On the force, in the police, as *"he looks jobby"*
John	Client of prostitute
Jumper	Someone who steals from offices
Ker-ching	Said after giving low-level caution etc just before end of a shift, ensuring significant overtime to do the paperwork (from sound of cash register)
Kremlin	New Scotland Yard. See also Cowards Castle
KSI	Killed and Seriously Injured
Lag	Frequent offender
Largee	Loot
LAS	London Ambulance Service
Late turn	Shift / tour of duty that starts at 2pm and ends at 10pm

Lay down	Plant false evidence
Legend	Cover story for undercover officer
Lid	Uniformed police person (from helmet)
Lift	(a) Arrest (Strathclyde) (b) Steal (c) Kidnap
Lilliwhites	HM Customs and Excise
Lion intoximeter	Machine used to measure amount of alcohol in the breath
LOB	Load of Bollocks; a call that didn't need a police presence
Local nick	Home police station
Lone ranger	Corrupt cop acting on his own
Market tester	Undercover cop purchasing from criminal suspect as part of a sting
Martini	Always sexually available, as *"Any time, any place, any where"*
Met	Metropolitan Police – covers London
Metcall	Centralised system that deals with all emergency calls to police in London and despatches local officers to area concerned

Metrocomicals	Met officers (Counties)
MIR	Major Investigation Room
Mister Wood	Truncheon
MIT	Major Investigation Team, works on specific murders & other serious and high profile crimes
MO	Modus Operandi. Methods a criminal tends to use as a habit
MOP	Member of the public
MP	Call sign for New Scotland Yard
MPA	Metropolitan Police Authority
M-Scan	Analyse for flammable materials
Muppet	(a) Most Useless Police Person Ever Trained (b) member of the public (c) Lay magistrate (d) DPS officer. See also Bench, Three monkeys, DPS
Musha	Pimp (Northern Counties)
Ned	Villain, yob, layabout, unsavoury character (Strathclyde)

NFA	(a) No Further Action (b) No Fixed Abode
NFCPA	No Further Cause Police Action
Nick	(a) Steal (b) Arrest (c) Police Station
Nights	Shift that runs from 10pm to 6am (Met)
Noble cause corruption	Bending or breaking the law in order to ensure a guilty verdict when the evidence may not be enough
NonDe	Nondescript, unmarked police vehicle
Nostrils	Sawn off shot-gun (obsolete)
Not carnival related	A bare-faced lie. Said to derive from the Notting Hill carnival press conferences, when all incidents of any kind were said to have no relation to the carnival
NPIA	(a) National Police Improvement Agency (b) No Point In Asking
NSY	New Scotland Yard
NTR	Nothing to Report
Numpty	Not a clever person
Nut	(a) Costs incurred by criminal preparing for a crime (b) Head (c) Hit with head

Nut and gut	Medical examination of a prisoner
Obbo	Observation, surveillance
Off-piste	Gone off the book, acting outside normal procedures and regulations
Office	Police station (CID)
Old Bill	Police. The origins of this name are obscure
Old lag	Offender in and out of jail
Old sweat	Long serving officer. See also Canteen Culture
Olympic flame, Olympic torch	Officer who never goes out
On his toes	Did a runner, escaped
On side	Corrupted, in a criminal's pocket
Onion	Sergeant (Rhyming slang, Onion Bhaji = Sargie)
Overshoot	Accusing a suspect of something so serious that they are happy to admit to a lesser crime

Overtime bandit	Officer who ensures as much work as possible goes beyond the end of a shift. See also Ker-ching.
PAC	Premises Appear Correct
PACE	Police and Criminal Evidence Act, the basis of many of the current rules that regulate police work
Padding	Adding to a drugs haul to make sure of a conviction
PADFAAU	Police Attended Did F*ck All As Usual
Panda (car)	Mobile patrol car. Derives from the old white Morris Minor cars formally used, now obsolete
PANTS	Police Are Not The Solution
PAX	Passenger
PC	Police Constable
PCSO	Police Community Support Officer. Uniformed civilian staff who support regular police officers and are viewed with appreciation or disdain. See also Blunkett's Babes, C-3P0, CHIMPS, Plastic Police

Peckham Rolex	Electronic tag worn by convicted criminals to monitor them outside prison
Peewee	Policewoman (Merseyside)
PESTELGO	Political, Environmental, Social/Demographics, Technological, Economic, Legal, Geographical, Organisational Issues (official police risk assessment criteria)
PI	Personal Injury
Pig	(a) Police (b) Polite, Intelligent Gentleman.
Pinch	(a) Arrest (b) Steal
Plainer	Plain clothes officer (Strathclyde)
Plastics, Plastic Police	Less than approving names for PCSOs
PLO	Prosecution Liaison Officer
PLONK	(a) Person of Little Or No Knowledge (b) Female Police Officer
PM	Post Mortem
PO	Police Officer
POLCOL	Police Collision
POLSA	Police Search Advisor

POP	(a) Problem Orientated Policing (b) Person On Premises
Potential customer	Suspect
PR	Personal Radio
Probationer	Rookie police officer in the first two years of service
Probby	Probationer
Prove	Murder, dispose of, terminate (Strathclyde)
Public bar	Police station reception (Strathclyde)
Pulled	(a) Stopped by police (b) Told off by senior officer
QE	Queen's Evidence. Evidence given against accomplice in the hope of getting a lighter sentence
QPM	Queen's Police Medal
QSR	Quality Service Report

Rammit	Battering ram for entering locked premises (Strathclyde) See Enforcer
Ramp	(a) Police search (b) Criminal scam.
Rat	Really Adept at Traffic law - traffic policeman, not a term of approval
Refs	Refreshment break, meal break (Met)
Regulation 163 Notice	Official notice that a police officer is being investigated for criminal behaviour
Relief	(a) Duty, shift (b) The officers on duty at a particular time (Met)
Relief bicycle	See Station bike
Resident informant	Supergrass
Richard	Yob (polite version of "dick")
Roll	Mug, steal from (Merseyside)
Roll over	Confess profusely (Merseyside)
RTA	Road Traffic Accident
RTC	Road Traffic Collision
RTI	Road Traffic Incident

Rubber heels	DPS officer
Runner	(a) Fugitive (b) Escape
Savvie up	Get together and synchronise notes prior to court appearance
SCD	Specialist Crime Directorate (runs major investigation teams)
Scribe	Someone delegated to write during an interview (prior to use of tape recorders)
Scrote	Villain
Section 25	Arrest powers under PACE if person gives false or no name and address
Section House	Living quarters for young single officers
Senga	Female yob (Strathclyde)
Serious Statement Taking Squad	Serious Crime Squad (Strathclyde)
Service confidence	Moving an officer to a "safe" job in cases when suspicions couldn't be proved
SFQ	Stupid F*cking Question

SFQJ	Silly F*cking Question Jacket (the Police-issue Hi Visibility jacket, allegedly because that's all you get when you wear it)
Shiny arse	Never goes out (trousers well polished by office chair)
Shoulder-surf	Observe pin numbers at cashpoints for use later with copied cards
Shout	Attending an incident, as *"going to a shout"*
Show out	Drop subtle hints that you are also an officer when stopped by fellow officer
Sign (someone) on	Take a person on as your personal informant
SIO	Senior Investigating Officer
Slag	(a) Criminal (b) Person whose sexual morality is in question
Slaggy	Like a slag (see above)
Slammer	Prison
Slaughter	Safe place for criminals to divide proceeds after a job
SNAFU	Situation Normal: All Fucked Up
Snitch, Snout	Informant
SOCO	Scene Of Crime Officer, in charge of gathering evidence. Now CSI

SOIE	Set Off In Error (as in an alarm)
Spice Girls	Territorial Support Group
Spin	Raid, search. See also Turn over, Drum
SPOC	Single Point Of Contact
SPOF	Single Point Of Failure
Station bike	Female officer said to be sexually available
Station cat	Officer who never goes out
Station Stamp	(a) Stamp used to validate correspondence, also used to stamp a new WPCs backside (b) Coffee stain on a statement
Stick	(Noun) Truncheon, term mainly used by older officers, as *"Sticks out!"* (Verb) *"After assessing the situation, I sticked him"*
Stick out	(a) Get out truncheon (b) Dangerous situation (c) Have your cover blown when in plain clothes
Stiff	Dead person
Stinger	Spikes for laying across road to puncture tyres of escaping cars. See also HOSTYDS

Stip, Stipe	Stipendiary magistrate
Stitch up	Ensure prosecution of a suspect through dubious means
Strawberry Mivvie	Civvie, civilian police staff. Can be shortened to Strawbs or Mivvie
Stretch	Sentence
Sud death	Sudden death
Suit	Plain clothes officer
Supergrass	A very important informer; high-level criminal or corrupt officer who has turned into a grass
Sus	Discredited law that allowed police to stop anyone *"on suspicion"* (obsolete)
Sweeney	Flying squad (rhyming slang: Sweeney Todd)
TA'd	Crashed (of car). From TA, Traffic Accident
TDA	Taken and Driven Away, car theft
Tea boy	Yob (Strathclyde)
Tea mobile	A tea boy's car (Strathclyde)

Tenure	Old practice of moving officers around rapidly from CID to uniform and back (Met)
TFF	Too F*cking Fast; over the speed limit
The Firm	CID (Met) See also Department
The Lump	Building site fraud to avoid payment of income tax
Thick and Stupid Group	Territorial Support Group
Thief taker	Term of praise for a police officer
Thieves	Metropolitan Police Officers, as designated by officers of other forces (Counties)
Three monkeys	Magistrate's bench
TIC	Taken Into Consideration – crimes confessed to in the hope of a lesser sentence
Ticket	Warrant, as *"Go get a ticket to spin his drum"*
TIE	Trace, Implicate or Eliminate
Time	Prison sentence
Tin tack	Get the sack
Tip up	Search someone (W Midlands)

Tit	Helmet - from the point at the top
Tom	Prostitute
Tout	(a) Informant (Strathclyde) (b) Illegal reseller of tickets (general)
TP	Test Purchaser, undercover cop in sting
Trumpton	Fire Brigade (from the 1960s Children's TV series)
TSG	Territorial Support Group (unit dedicated to dealing with public order from potential violent incidents to riots)
Turn	8 hour shifts starting respectively 6am, 2pm & 10pm or 7am, 3pm & 11pm (Met)
Turn over	Search. See also Spin, Drum
Turn tricks	Sell sexual favours
Turtles	Gloves - (rhyming slang: turtle doves)
TWOC	Take Without Owners Consent
Twocer	Thief, particularly of cars

UC	Undercover Cop
Uniform	Uniformed officer
Uniform carrier	Useless or ineffective police officer.
Upstairs	Crown court, where the dock is reached by climbing up stairs from the cells
Verbal	Put false self-incriminating words in suspect's mouth; falsely incriminating statement made up by police officer
VHF	Radio system carried in each car; operates on VHF frequency and is direct line to HQ
VIW	(a) Vulnerable and Intimidated Witness (b) Victim Informant Witness
VPU	Vulnerable Prisoner Unit, used to keep prisoners likely to be victimised by other prisoners
Warrant card	Proof of a Police Officer's identity and authority
White stuff	Milk, important ingredient of a police officer's favourite hot drink
Window licker	Psychotic, deranged person

Window warrior	Prisoner who constantly shouts from his cell window
Wire	(a) Wire tap on phone, etc (b) Recorder taped to body of undercover officer
WOFTAM	Waste Of F*cking Time And Money
Woodentop, Woodie	Uniformed police, from the traditional helmet that used to be made of wood
Woolly backs	County police (Merseyside)
Wrap	Small bag of cocaine or other drugs
YOI	Young Offenders Institute
Zombie	Disliked prison officer, as *"more dead than alive"*
Zoomer	Person who's off their head on narcotics

OTHER TITLES AVAILABLE

Language Glossaries
American English/English American
Australian English/English Australian
Cumbrian English
Gay slang
Geordie English
Hip Hop English
Home Counties English
Irish English/English Irish
Lancashire English
Military Slang
Playground Slang & Teenspeak
Police Slang
Prison Slang
Rhyming Cockney Slang
Rude Rhyming Slang
Scottish English/English Scottish
Scouse English

West Country English
Yiddish English/English Yiddish

Yorkshire English

History
The Death of Kings – A history of how the Kings
& Queens of England died

Who's Buried Where?

Literary Quiz & Puzzle Books
Bronte Sisters
Gilbert & Sullivan
Shakespeare
Thomas Hardy

Charles Dickens
Jane Austen
Sherlock Holmes

All of these titles area available from good booksellers
or by contacting the publisher:
Abson Books London 5 Sidney Square London E1 2EY
Tel 020 7790 4737 Fax 020 7790 7346
email absonbooks@aol.com
web www.absonbooks.co.uk